Your
Set Time
—— FOR ——
Marriage

Your Set Time For Marriage

All Scriptures are from the King James Version (KJV).

ISBN: 978-1-63308-216-8 (paperback)
         978-1-63308-217-5 (ebook)

Interior and Cover Design by R'tor John D. Maghuyop

CHALFANT ECKERT
PUBLISHING

1028 S Bishop Avenue, Dept. 178
Rolla, MO 65401

Printed in United States of America

KWESI FRIMPONG

Your Set Time —— FOR —— *Marriage*

THE POWER OF TESTIMONIES ON MARRIAGE

CHALFANT ECKERT

PUBLISHING

I dedicate this book to God who brought my out of shame and disgrace. Took me out of being single into marriage. My sweet and loving wife, Mrs Adejoke Yaa Favour Adeniyi, who showed me love and enormous encouragement beyond all odds. Indeed every good and perfect gift comes from God. This book was made possible because of her. I love you .My kids who are very supporting in all ways- Victoria, Irenen, and Deborah, David and Davida. Lastly to the this commission, winners chapel international. who injected supernatural faith into me and made me believe that I can do all things through Christ who strengthen me.

TABLE OF CONTENTS

ACKNOWLEDGEMENT 7

INTRODUCTION 9

CHAPTER ONE: Purpose Of This Epistle ... 15

CHAPTER TWO: Marriage 19

CHAPTER THREE: Reasons A Man Takes
                A Wife 31

CHAPTER FOUR: The Testimonies 41

CHAPTER FIVE: Habits Of A Happy
                Relationship 53

YOUR SET TIME IS NOW! 59

ACKNOWLEDGEMENT

Bishop David O Oyedepo
*Founder And President Of
Winners Chapel International*

My Wife-Mrs Adejoke Yaa Favor Adeniyi

Victoria, Irene And Deborah Okyere.

Dr. Kitty Bickford
President Of This Publication.

All My Spiritual Patents

INTRODUCTION

*And they overcame him by the blood of the
Lamb, and by the word of their testimony.*
Revelation 12:11

Beloved, one of the weapons to destroy the works of the enemy is testimonies. To overcome life issues and prevail, you need the testimonies of what God has done for others and for you. David tapped into the testimony of what God did for him in the wilderness, in the bush. He remembered what God did for him and that allowed him through faith to overcome Goliath.

*David said moreover, The LORD that
delivered me out of the paw of the
lion, and out of the paw of the bear, he
will deliver me out of the hand of this
Philistine. And Saul said unto David,
Go, and the LORD be with thee.*
1 Samuel 17:37

Come on! Testimonies are prophetic, and they repeat themselves in our lives.

Are you of marriage age and no suitor is coming forward? Are you marriage material? Do you desire to get married so you can enjoy the favor of God?

He who finds a wife finds a good thing,
And obtains favour from the Lord.
Proverbs 18:22

Marrying early is beneficial. A lot of us think we are getting old because our friends are getting married, and we are not. Others may say that you are getting old, may mock you for being late to wed, and ask when you are getting married. The timing of your marriage should not be based on peer pressure, the calendar, or parental influence. Do not enter into marriage for any of these reasons. Beloved, move into marriage for the purposes of love and understanding.

Greater love hath no man than this, that
a man lay down his life for his friends.
John 15:13

Jesus came down to the earth to give the world love. Go into marriage with the spirit of *agape*, which is selfless love and respect. You must also weigh yourself to see if you are truly marriage material. Are you ready you leave your family and your single way of life, and to cleave to only your wife or your husband? God is ready to give you your partner, but the question is: Are you ready to receive that partner?

Give not that which is holy unto the dogs, neither cast ye your pearls before swine, lest they trample them under their feet, and turn again and rend you.
Matthew 7:6

Careful. Check yourself. This book will unravel a lot of secrets to you that will catapult you to your next level of miracle marriage. Remember that marriage was not man's idea, it was God himself who saw the need for man to have a companion, so God created marriage to solve that problem of loneliness. You shall be gloriously married after reading this book.

Every marital spell is being broken now as you read this book, in Jesus name. Whatever is not permitted in heaven is not allowed in your life. Marriage is permitted, and it is part of your redemptive package, so take now.

And they overcame him by the blood of the Lamb, and by the word of their testimony; and they loved not their lives unto the death.
Revelation 12:11

One of the ways to overcome the works of the devil is by the words of biblically-based testimonies. Open your mouth and tell the world what the Lord has for you and by so doing, you will be shaking the camp of the enemy. Bishop David Oyedepo (founder and presiding bishop over *Winners Chapel International* and *Living Faith Church World Wide)* said, "a closed mouth is a closed destiny." As you continually share little testimonies and thank God for them, greater testimonies will come your way. This year, your miracle marriage testimony will emerge.

This book contains diverse, amazing, raw but proven testimonies of men and women of the faith from around the world. It is my prayer that as you read them, the miracles will be repeated in your personal life, in Jesus precious name.

Whatever is confronting you and creating an obstacle to your progress in marriage will be overcome and terminated by these amazing testimonies. Read them prayerfully, meditatively, and thoughtfully, and your life will never be the same. As you walk through this journey of testimonies, may your life be full of testimonies. May your suitor locate you right now wherever you are, in Jesus precious name! Shout a louder Amen!

CHAPTER ONE

———————————————

Purpose Of This Epistle

The purpose of this book is to help you understand what testimonies can do and what they have done in other people's lives, so they can reproduce in your life if you desire.

The righteousness of thy testimonies is everlasting: give me understanding, and I shall live.
Psalm 119:144

Testimonies are as potent as the Word of God. In fact, David overcame Goliath by shooting arrows of testimonies at him,

34 And David said unto Saul, Thy servant kept his father's sheep, and there came a lion, and a bear, and took a lamb out of the flock:

³⁵ And I went out after him, and smote
him, and delivered it out of his mouth: and
when he arose against me, I caught him by
his beard, and smote him, and slew him.
³⁶ Thy servant slew both the lion and the
bear: and this uncircumcised Philistine
shall be as one of them, seeing he hath
defied the armies of the living God.
³⁷ David said moreover, The Lord that
delivered me out of the paw of the
lion, and out of the paw of the bear, he
will deliver me out of the hand of this
Philistine. And Saul said unto David,
Go, and the Lord be with thee.
1 Samuel 17:34-37

Every day is for God but the day you
believe is for you. If you believe, you will
be the next in line to share your marital
testimony. Jesus is Lord.

Even today, we still overcome by
testimonies.

And they overcame him by the blood of the
Lamb, and by the word of their testimony;
and they loved not their lives unto the death.
Revelation 12:11

You are overcoming every singleness and every marital stagnation now as you digest this epistle of diverse turnaround testimonies and miracle marriages. This is because every testimony of Jesus is prophetic and is the spirit of Jesus.

And I fell at his feet to worship him. And he said unto me, See thou do it not: I am thy fellowservant, and of thy brethren that have the testimony of Jesus: worship God: for the testimony of Jesus is the spirit of prophecy.
Revelation 19:10

The testimony of Jesus is the Holy Spirit proving that He will not be taken away from the world. Today we still testify about Jesus by this same Holy Ghost. Today we still have the testimonies of Jesus dying and resurrecting from the death. Death could not hold him captive in the grave. He has risen from the death and is seated at the right hand of God the Father in heaven. What a testimony we have as the anchor of our Christianity. Remember without this great truth, there wouldn't have been Christ preached.

You are the next to share your testimony. Only believe. The God, who did it for others, will do it for you. Jesus is Lord.

CHAPTER TWO

Marriage

Marriage from a biblical point of view is a divine institutional covenant, a union between man and woman which is ordained by God. It is an institution ordained and ordered by God. It is the only institution that was established before sin entered into man. Marriage was the first institution created by God. Whenever you start talking about marriage, home, and family, God gets involved. The joining together of the husband and the wife is the smallest cell of the church: two people who love God coming together as one.

Marriage is divine because it is from and of God. It is a covenant because it is an agreement between God, a man, and a woman.

...and a threefold cord is
not quickly broken.
Ecclesiastes 4:12

Your Father in heaven cares about your
comfort so much that he made marriage
available to you. Being alone is not part
of your inheritance. From today, you shall
not be alone.

And the Lord God said, It is not good
that the man should be alone; I will
make him an help meet for him.
Genesis 2:18

God's work would not have been
completed without marriage. There would
not have been reproduction of His kind if
Adam had been left alone. He made a help
meet for man to enable him to propagate
his kind, a help meet suitable to man
intellectually, morally, and physically as his
counterpart. Marriage is God's institution
for man, but you need to know who He has
ordained for you.

You are not complete without marriage. As you read this book, I see you entering into your miracle marriage right now, in Jesus name. You can never be alone. That man or that woman ordained to make you complete is coming to you. Marriage is your redemptive right as a Christian.

Marriage is honourable in all,
and the bed undefiled...
Hebrews 13:4

Marriage is the greatest institution ordained by God himself, the first family instituted by God himself from heaven. You are ordained to marry. You are destined to get your miracle marriage.

Where there is anything designed, there is a designer. Whether it's a truck, building, or train—or even marriage—there is always a mastermind behind the masterpiece. Marriage is the full expression and design of God's image in human beings.

In Genesis we read:

*[18] And the Lord God said, It is not good
that the man should be alone; I will
make him an help meet for him.
[21] And the Lord God caused a deep
sleep to fall upon Adam, and he
slept: and he took one of his ribs, and
closed up the flesh instead thereof;
[22] And the rib, which the Lord God had
taken from man, made he a woman,
and brought her unto the man.*
Genesis 2:18, 21, 22

Your partner is being brought to you
now, in Jesus name. The Bible said He
brought Eve to Adam as wife. God was the
first to officiate a wedding.

Why did God do it that way? Why create
one being and then take a part of that being
and create a second? God differentiated yet
made woman complementary to the man.

*And Adam said, This is now bone
of my bones, and flesh of my flesh:*

she shall be called Woman, because
she was taken out of Man.
Genesis 2:23

Woman was made a being who is sexually, emotionally and in other ways different, yet of man's substance? Upon seeing her, Adam might have observed, "It's me . . . But not me." Well, if you think about it, it does sound like the kind of thing you might expect the Trinity to do.

Everything you need is inside of you. Your wife, marriage, everything you can think of is in you. Look deep within yourself and you will see it. By looking deep, I mean meditating on God's Word and seeing your wife through God's divine eyes. Your rib, the bone of your bone, and flesh of your flesh. Eve was in Adam, so as Adam got closer to God, God told him to sleep, and He would bring out a wife to be Adam's companion. As you get closer to God, as you see God, He will bring your woman out of you. She is your rib; she is there. He did for Adam, for me, and for others, and He will do it for you.

Your partner is right with you and in
you. It's time to get married, yes; the set
time is now. The Trinity (Father, Son, and
Holy Spirit) is a family, and thus man in
God's image must be made a family as well.
Therefore, a man cannot completely realize
the essence of his existence until he learns
to exist with someone and for someone.
Both relationship and communion are
crucial to this process.

We see from Genesis 1 and 2 that God
created woman from the side of man so
that the man would not be alone. You are
not meant to be alone. Get your man or
get your woman and be complete. When
you meet your rib, you will always radiate,
glow, and be joyous. When Adam saw Eve,
he must have been overjoyed for she was
the bone of his bone and the flesh of his
flesh. He would have been happy at once.
You are sad because you are alone. When
Adam was alone, he may have been quiet,
sad, and had no one to talk to, socialize
with, share or discuss issues. But when Eve
came, it boosted his happiness and made
his life better.

New Testament saints teach us that God created the church from the side of the second Adam—Christ—for the same reason—for intimate fellowship. No man is an island. God did not make us to be islands unto ourselves. In fact, scripture tells us:

Come now, and let us reason together, saith the Lord: though your sins be as scarlet, they shall be as white as snow; though they be red like crimson, they shall be as wool.
Isaiah 1:18

God is a fellowshipping God, who always wants to socialize with us, talk to us, and reason with us, so He made man in his own image and in his likeness. We have the Spirit of God. We exhibit the Spirit of God. We have the DNA of God. It is only Satan that walks alone. You are not Satan, and you cannot be alone.

When Eve was left alone, the devil entered, and that was how sin entered into the world. You see, loneliness is not good. It can lead to evil. You will marry, in Jesus name.

Back in the Genesis account, we note that the newly created Eve was Adam—his very flesh and bone, and for that reason, the Bible says:

> *And Adam said, This is now bone*
> *of my bones, and flesh of my flesh:*
> *she shall be called Woman, because*
> *she was taken out of Man.*
> *Therefore shall a man leave his father*
> *and his mother, and shall cleave unto*
> *his wife: and they shall be one flesh.*
> Genesis 2:23-24

Without leaving, there will not be cleaving. For you to able to cleave to your partner, there must be leaving. Leave certain things behind. Things you do when you are alone will be different from things you will do when you want to be two joined together as one flesh. Leave the *boyism* for *manism*. Boys and girls don't get married. It takes a woman or a man to marry. Leave fear and have faith.

> *…the just shall live by faith…*
> Hebrews 10:38

You will marry by faith, not fear. If you fear in the days of adversity, your strength is small. Be the man or woman God has ordained you to be.

There are more than one ways of leaving which include:

1. Physically leaving a specific location. You can't be in your parents' house and expect to get married. If you are in a single room, think of getting an apartment immediately when you find a woman.
2. Economic/financial leaving involves good financial standing.
3. Leaving old habits. Follow the good direction and counsel of parents and extended family, close friends concerning the opposite sex.
4. Leaving poor communication skills behind. Know how to relate to the opposite sex when you marry. Let your spouse know all about you. If you are a secret person, learn to be open. Prepare yourself very well before you enter. You are blessed.

Leaving and cleaving is a critical concept that you must know and exercise if you are to really love your mate in a covenant relationship. Some people never get around to leaving parents. The apron strings are still tied, and Mama is still helping her little child make decisions. When you leave home to get married, it's time to cut the apron strings. Leave Mama's influence and control over your life when you join yourself to your mate. There is a leaving, and then there is a cleaving. This means as a husband and wife, you are drawn together apart and must leave behind all romantic relationships from the past.

A husband and a wife are to cleave to each other. If you cleave, it won't be as easy to leave each other. God calls you to become one flesh in marriage, has called two to become one, to be united in attitude, mind, vision, and direction. This is why singles need to come to a unity of mind and heart before they marry. Many people simply come to a unity in the physical relationship. but never come to unity in their minds, vision, direction, intention, and purpose in life. Many people get married and later discover that the person they married has a different plan for life. Plan, prepare, and know yourself before you enter into marriage.

CHAPTER THREE

Reasons A Man Takes A Wife

Because woman was originally a constituent part of man, she must return to become one with him again do that the full expression and design of God's image in human beings can be revealed. You are returning to your partner now, in Jesus name. You will not be alone forever; you will surely get your wife or your husband. There is a reason you came as a man or woman.

> *And the Lord God said, It is not good that the man should be alone; I will make him an help meet for him.*
> Genesis 2:18

God commanded Adam to be under subjection to God's rules:

*¹⁶ And the Lord God commanded
the man, saying, Of every tree of the
garden thou mayest freely eat:
¹⁷ But of the tree of the knowledge
of good and evil, thou shalt not eat
of it: for in the day that thou eatest
thereof thou shalt surely die.*
Genesis 2: 16-17

God is also a good friend and a father
who will always want the best for his
children. You are not alone.

Reason 1: Companionship

God made the woman to be with the man
as a companionship. Adam was lonely.
He had everything in the world he could
possibly need, but there was a loneliness
- an emptiness on the inside of him that
wasn't satisfied. Eve had to come and fill
that need. She completed Adam, just
as God has created wives to complete
husbands today.

When God brought Eve to Adam, he
started rapping that she was "bone of my

bone and the flesh of my flesh; she shall be called woman because she was taken out of man."

The God who made us knows us and what is good for us more than we ourselves know. It is not good for man to be alone thus, loneliness is not for our comfort, for man is a sociable creature. It is pleasurable to man to exchange knowledge and affection with one his kind, to inform and to be informed, to love and to be loved.

> *⁹ Two are better than one; because they have a good reward for their labour.*
> *¹⁰ For if they fall, the one will lift up his fellow: but woe to him that is alone when he falleth; for he hath not another to help him up.*
> Ecclesiastes 4:9-10

If there be but one man in the world, what melancholy he needs be; perfect solitude would have turned a paradise into a desert, and a palace into a dungeon.

Whatever man does, he still needs someone to help him. God said, "Let us make man." Even in creation, God desired assistance. You can't be alone; you are not meant to be alone. Your bone of bone is coming to you by the time you finish reading this book. Receive it now. Your companion is on the way.

God has made one of your kind, one of your nature, of the same rank of being; one for you to cohabit with.

And the Lord God said, It is not good that the man should be alone; I will make him an help meet for him.
Genesis 2:18

We have need of one another's help for we are members of one another.

For as the body is one, and hath many members, and all the members of that one body, being many are one body: so also is Christ.
1 Corinthians 12:12

The relationship with a woman is likely to be comfortable when meekness directs and determines choice, and mutual helpfulness is the constant effort and endeavor.

33 But he that is married careth for the things that are of the world, how he may please his wife.
34 There is difference also between a wife and a virgin. The unmarried woman careth for the things of the Lord, that she may be holy both in body and in spirit: but she that is married careth for the things of the world, how she may please her husband.
1 Corinthians 7:33-34

Reason 2: To be a Help Meet

And the Lord God said, It is not good that the man should be alone; I will make him an help meet for him.
Genesis 2:18

Help meet means the woman is helpful to her husband in many ways: to pray with him, to give him physical pleasure through sex, to nourish him with tasty food, to encourage him when he is struggling, to comfort him when he is sad or hurt, to counsel him with Godly wisdom, to show him and his friends and family hospitality, to care for his home, to help him in all ways, and to be his social companion.

Reason 3: To Avoid Fornication

If you desire to get married, stay away from fornication. Wait for your wedding night to be intimate with your bride. You should not be having sex with a woman before you are married to her. You can't be holding onto something with one hand and expect to receive something with the other hand.

Why buy the cow when the milk is free? Ladies who are staying with boys remember this: No man will spend money to seek your hand in marriage when you are giving him the sexual benefits of marriage without the wedding ring. If your breast is available to your man every day, why get in a hurry to marry you? Think about it.

Now concerning the things whereof
ye wrote unto me: It is good for a
man not to touch a woman.
² Nevertheless, to avoid fornication, let
every man have his own wife, and let
every woman have her own husband.
1 Corinthians 7:1-2

Reason 4: To Have Children

²⁶ And God said, Let us make man in our
image, after our likeness: and let them have
dominion over the fish of the sea, and over
the fowl of the air, and over the cattle, and
over all the earth, and over every creeping
thing that creepeth upon the earth.
²⁷ So God created man in his own image,
in the image of God created he him;
male and female created he them.
²⁸ And God blessed them, and God said
unto them, Be fruitful, and multiply, and
replenish the earth, and subdue it: and
have dominion over the fish of the sea,
and over the fowl of the air, and over every
living thing that moveth upon the earth.
Genesis 1:26-28

Please note that it is not the arrival of children that validates the marriage nor the absence of that nullify your marriage.

Lo, children are an heritage of the LORD:
and the fruit of the womb is his reward.
Psalm 127:3

The following chapter will present the testimonies of some couples for which God gave miracle marriages, or restored and united couples whose marriages were on the rocks. No matter the condition of your marriage (or being single), God is capable of bringing your partner to you and also of restoring your marriage. If God has done it for others and He is the same yesterday, today and forever, then He can do it for you, too!

Meditate on these testimonies with faith believing God for your perfect help meet. Testimonies are as potent as the Word of God. Every marital spell is shattered by the anointing right now. You are gloriously getting your companion, in

Jesus name. You are due for settlement, at last; marriage shall be your testimony.!

Jesus is Lord, Glory to God

CHAPTER FOUR

The Testimonies

And they overcame him by the blood of the
Lamb, and by the word of their testimony;
and they loved not their lives unto the death.
Revelation 12:11

My Testimony

My marriage was in itself a testimony that I could never forget. I had said to myself that I wanted to marry a fair woman many years ago, not knowing God's plan and purpose for me. God had prepared a vessel that I did not know: a virtuous, industrious, wise and wonderful woman. After a series of broken relationships that spanned years, God finally settled me with the bone of bone and the flesh of my flesh. I waited for God, and my package came with my name written on it. God caused my wife to

come from the United States through an
Aunty. I had not previously met or known
this woman. As God brought Eve and
she was perfect for Adam, so my wife was
perfect when I saw her for the first time at
Kotoka International Airport. I knew that
she was a gift indeed from God. Full of
wisdom and beauty, she brought me the
completeness I was seeking, and because
of her, I wrote this book. We got married
without delay in March 21st, 2014. Since
then our marriage has been from glory to
glory. I got married after years of wanting
the right woman, and if God did it for me,
He could also do it for you. You will also
get married. It doesn't matter your age,
background, or knowledge. The God, who
did it for my wife, and I will do it for you.
Glory to God.

Miracle Marriage at 55 Years Old!

"I believed God for a marital breakthrough.
I attended Shiloh since 1999, and every
time I came, among other requests was to be
connected to my life partner. God answered
other requests except that singular one.

To the shame of the devil, in Shiloh 2012, the prophetic word was fulfilled in my life. On October 26 this year, I got connected, and I am happily married at 55 years old. To God be the glory!"

Janet Abu, Nigeria

Miracle Marriage and Deliverance from Death!

"When we were concluding our marriage seminar, the bwishop came to our class and told us that he would go with us. He kept saying it. And I believed it. The bishop prayed for us on the 2nd of February, and then on the 4th, we embarked on the journey to the east for our traditional wedding, which took place on the 8th.

So while we were back there in the East, a Brother friend of ours called us, saying that he saw us in a revelation, and he instructed that when we are coming back to Lagos, we should not take the same vehicle and that we should not let people know about our trip, and we should also pray against the spirit of death.

So, we finished our engagement and the next day which was on the 9th, being Sunday we boarded a bus from Port Harcourt. God showed me a scripture from Psalm 106:8 that he would deliver us. *(Nevertheless he saved them for his name's sake, that he might make his mighty power to be known.)*

While on the journey, I received a strange call on my phone from a woman. When the woman heard my voice, she cut the call. As I was trying to call her back, one of the front tires of the bus went off the wheel, and the bus started swerving. After some seconds, it started somersaulting.

When the bus finally stopped, about six people were already dead, and I was sitting in the front seat. I came out by myself without a single scratch on my body. I picked out my bag and started making phone calls.

The devil thought that we would not marry, but God has joined us gloriously in holy matrimony! I give all the glory to the God of this commission!"

Mr. and Mrs. Maurice Chukwu

Marital Breakthrough

"Praise God. I have been trusting God for marital breakthrough and a federal government job. I attended miracle marriage service for the month of May 2012 at Goshen as an onlooker but when I heard people's testimonies after that miracle marriage service that month of May 2012, I was challenged. During the month of August, I came well prepared. I even came with an engagement ring, a point of contact. Brother Mrs. Abioye gave us 90 days for the manifestation of our miracles. To the glory of God, that same day I was proposed to by my God-ordained spouse. And the wedding came up June 2013. This can only be God. Thank you, sir. To God alone be all the glory."

Franca A.

Life Partner Came

"I want to thank the God of this commission for answering my earnest heart's desire. I'm a member of this commission and worship at Goshen, but now in Nigerian Law School-Lagos campus for my bar Part ii. I've believed God for a life partner, not just a wife but a virtuous one after God's heart for me. During last year prayer and fasting and in one of the Sunday services at Goshen, Bishop Abioye declared that it was our covenant miracle marriage service and said that all eligible singles should come at the altar area and dance and praise God as if we were dancing in our traditional marriage. As a man, I felt somehow as to how I would come out and be seen by people because it is common belief that only sisters are in need for divine intervention for marriage but right inside me, I knew I needed God's help in this wise more than ever. The spirit God told me to go out. We came out, danced and praised God, after which the bishop prayed for us and said that, "From my heart as a father, I bless you and declare your long-awaited partner to locate you before long, in Jesus name." He also said we should be sensitive and open our eyes. I keyed into all the declarations. On 3rd June 2012, while away with my boss in South Africa for a vacation, God miraculously connected me with my covenant virtuous wife, who at that time was in Port Harcourt, Nigeria and today to the glory of God, we're happily married. The God of this commission is alive and to God alone be all the glory."

Brother Victor E.

Marital Spell Destroyed

"I joined this commission 2012. At Shiloh 2011, I heard a testimony of how God destroyed a marital spell in a family and how 11 members of the family got married that year. I was amazed, and I keyed into it in 2012. I attended the miracle marriage service in 2013; the bishop said God told him to lay hands on everyone.

While at the viewing center I stretched my hands towards the screen, placed them

on my forehead and believed my case was
settled. To the glory of God shortly after
that service, my sister met her husband
in June 2013, and they got married in
October 2013 at the age of 40. Also in
February 2014, I was colorfully married.
Praise the Lord!"

Many Months of Marital Separation Restored

"After many months of being separated
from my husband, I surrendered my
desperation to be back together to God.
Once I gave it to Him, he worked through
me to restore my marriage. My husband
kept telling me the only way he could
forgive me was to divorce me. I knew this
was not God's will and with hard work,
we could work through this. God was so
faithful and has brought us back together!
God is good all the time! My steadfast will
to stand became stronger along with my
faith in God. It's not easy to stand but the
happiness it brings, in the end, is worth
every tear. Glory to God."

3 Years Marital Separation Restored

"It was three years back when my husband left his marital home with a one-year-old child in my hands to support. I struggled as a single parent to keep this child in good state for three years. I came to this service on the last day of the month of September; that was 27th September 2015, which was a thanksgiving service and covenant day of recovery and sat down at the hope entrance believing God for speed recovery of my marital dignity. While the prophetic word was going forth, God's servant declared that "your runaway husband wherever he is shall return to you with speed this week." I shouted, "Amen!" to that declaration because that was my word for the day. I reached home after church service, and whiles cooking, my senior brother came telling me that my husband's car was parked in the yard. Immediately rushed out, lo and behold, my husband was sitting in the car with all his belongings, and he said to me, "Sweetheart, I have finally come home." I return all to the God of this commission for taking away my shame and reproach among men and restoring my home."

Dede K.

Marital Delay Terminated

"I joined this commission in November 2011. During Shiloh 2012, I prayed that the yoke of marital delay in my family will be destroyed because none of my brothers and sisters were married. On the third night which was tagged 'night of settlement,' God answered my prayers. On October 26th, 2013, two of my sisters got married. Furthermore, on November 26th, my brother also got married. Afterward, the devil attacked my family. On our way home after the wedding, we had an accident, and the car somersaulted. However, we came out unhurt. I thank the God of Shiloh for his faithfulness! Praise the Lord."

Henry Akeme-Abuja

Marital Siege Broken

"When Bishop David Oyedepo declared
the 2nd phase of *Operation Rescue*
prophetic agenda, I engaged in it fully on
morning raids. That week I invited a lady
to the marital banquet Sunday. She had
lost hope in marriage and in men. I told
her to come because I know God will do
something great for her. She asked if I was
married, and I said, "No." I told her my
marital issues would be settled tomorrow.
On that marital breakthrough banquet,
Bishop David Oyedepo declared and
prophesied that some of us will receive a
proposal that same day. Like magic, I got
home and got a message from a business
contact who has not called me for a long
while. I tried to discuss business with him,
but he told me, "It's you I am interested in
now, not business." He proposed marriage
to me that same day. Meanwhile, the lady
I invited to service also called to share her
testimony that on the Monday after the

marital breakthrough banquet she got a proposal. I believed the word of God's servant and received my portion. God of wonder double is indeed a rewarder. Praise the Lord." Anita C. Odiaka

CHAPTER FIVE

Habits Of A Happy Relationship

L et me quickly take you through some habits of a good relationship.

1. Settle disputes peacefully.

When you feel anger, avoid saying or yelling words you can't take back. Instead have a planned agreement that you each will back away.

2. Spend quality time together.

Make time for each other. With busy schedules, we often forget to relax and enjoy others. Two people can be right next to each other, yet miles apart. Ignoring someone often hurts more than angry words! Carve out special time at least once a week for just the two of you.

3. *Appreciate and help each other grow.*

Having an open appreciation for your significant other leads to a productive, fulfilling and peaceful union. Cheer for their victories. Celebrate their accomplishments, and encourage their goals and ambitions! Challenge them to be the best they can be.

4. *Live with integrity.*

Trust in each other and know you haven't been used or taken advantage of. Trust creates inner peace and security. Lies fester, but the truth heals or prevents trouble. Live daily with fairness, integrity, and reliability.

5. *Be loyal and devoted.*

True love and real friendship aren't about being inseparable. Love is about two people being true to each other even when they are separated. When it comes to relationships, remaining faithful is never an option, but a priority. Loyalty is everything.

6. *Love and respect each other as individuals.*

Our first and last love is self-love. Don't rely on your significant other, or anyone else, for your happiness and self-worth. Only you can be responsible for that. If you can't love and respect yourself, no one else will be able to either.

7. *Lend support during the good times and bad.*

Be there through the good, bad, happy, and sad times, too. Trust that you can count on each other, and be available not only when it's convenient, but when it's needed most even if inconvenient.

8. *Understand that every relationship is different.*

Don't compare your relationship to anyone else's relationship, especially that random couple whose relationship seems perfect.

Every couple makes their own love rules, love agreements, and love habits. Just focus on you two, and make your relationship the best it can be!

9. *Emphasize communication and listening.*

No one is a mind reader so your partner won't be able to figure out how you're feeling. Be specific and clear with yourself on what you want and make an effort to discover what your partner's needs are.

10. *Turn negatives into positives.*

Problems in a relationship can be broken down into numbers. If you're both honest with each other and with yourselves, logically look at the negatives and calmly list them. Work together as a team to tackle each negative, one by one.

11. *Be thoughtful every day.*

People who are in successful relationships nourish their partnerships regularly. They don't set their life on cruise control. Ask yourself, "What can I do today to make my partner's life better?" Little bits of effort every day will accumulate over time and make a big difference.

12. Set Realistic expectations.

Real relationships aren't what you see in the movies. They happen because each person values the other and is willing to make an investment of time into the partnership. They understand that not all days are passionate and romantic and that rough spots will require good communication.

YOUR SET TIME
IS NOW!

No matter what things look like right now, there is a quickening power of testimonies of God flowing to you right now!

Now I pray for you in the name of Jesus Christ, the name that is above every name. I curse every marital spell, enchantment, marital curse, disappointment, broken heart, and marital torment, in the name of Jesus!

Freedom of marriage is yours for the taking. It is part of your redemptive package.

Remember God is too faithful to fail! He is dependable, and He is more than enough. Your marital testimony is sure! Jesus saves!

Friend you can't receive the gift if you don't love and accept the giver of the gift.

Are you born again? Do you know Jesus? Does He live in your life?

Pray this prayer with me, by simply saying:

Father,
I come to you today in the name of
Jesus Christ. I believe that Jesus died on the
cross for my sins. I believe that He shed
his blood to wipe away my sins. Now I
receive Jesus into my life, right now, in Jesus
Name. Thank you, Lord, for saving me.
Amen.

If you said this prayer with me, believe that you are born again.

Therefore if any man be in Christ, he
is a new creature: old things are passed
away; behold, all things are become new.
2 Corinthians 5:17

New things are happening to you right now. Receive your marital breakthrough now! You are the next in line to share your testimony.

You are blessed!

Jesus loves you.

*M*arriage is good but it's for people who are prepared. Knowledge and preparation is needed for everything in life. If you don't see where you are going, you cant get there. The entrance of God's word brings light. If you are looking to get a good marriage, prepare.

Get in touch with us and will help you to counsel you in all areas to help you get and enjoy the best of marriage in your life. Don't cry again on how to choose a life partner. It is better to enjoy marriage than to endure marriage. Don't waste any more time. Be free from any stagnation and get help. Jesus is Lord. You are the next in line for a marriage testimony.

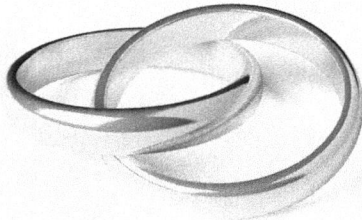

CALL NOW ON THE FOLLOWING NUMBERS
+16465750997 | +233205108678